Artistic Inspirations

6 Original Piano Solos Inspired by Masterpieces of Art

by Naoko Ikeda

ISBN 978-1-4803-8378-4

WILLIS MUSIC

EXCLUSIVELY DISTRIBUTED BY

Hal•Leonard®
CORPORATION

7777 W. BLUEMOUND RD. P.O. BOX 13819 MILWAUKEE, WI 53213

Visit Hal Leonard Online at
www.halleonard.com

PERFORMANCE NOTES

VALSE INNOCENT
Inspired by the *Progress of Love* series (1771-72) by Jean-Honoré Fragonard and *The Arts and Sciences* series (1750-52) by François Boucher

Rococo art is representative of French aristocratic tastes. In the paintings, children of nobility play in a picturesque court garden. The piece begins with a springy triple-time beat. Play with elegance at the key change in the middle section, and finish the piece with a grandiose, operatic gesture.

THE JUNGLE
Inspired by *The Sleeping Gypsy* (1897) by Henri Rousseau and several of his "jungle" paintings

An afternoon in the jungle passes slowly, almost listlessly. This is expressed by the constant rhythmic drumming in the left hand. The melody in the right hand describes animals in the thick greenery, colorful birds, and an observant human being. Note the precise pedal changes which signify the changing humidity in the jungle.

DANSE EN ROSE
Inspired by *Class de danse* (1879) by Edgar Degas

In ballet class they are learning new choreography. The lesson begins in a piano accompaniment style. The key change signifies that the dancer is now a star prima donna on center stage accompanied with a full orchestra of her imaginations. Play the staccatos clearly. Towards the end she returns slowly back to the reality of the ballet rehearsal room. Keep a steady rhythm as you dance through the piece.

NOCTURNE OF THE STARS
Inspired by *The Starry Night* (1889) and *Cypresses* (1889) by Vincent van Gogh

The great Van Gogh was able to condense emotion onto a canvas that reflected exactly who he was – undulating, intense, yet also very delicate. Dazzling stars shine above a blustery night wind, and the cypress trees strain to reach those stars. Play the final arpeggio like a sudden, unexpected gust of wind.

JOYFUL LOVE
Inspired by *The Lovers* (1913-14), *Birthday* (1915) and various stained glass windows by Marc Chagall

In this piece, the key of E Major represents a glowing spiritual happiness, while G Major embodies a joyful romantic love. In the variation section at M.18, both worlds combine merrily.

DREAMY HUES
Inspired by *New Harmony* (1936) by Paul Klee

"Various things exist in chaos and remain asleep within. They appear when the heart is touched."

Start quietly. As the melody and harmony gradually moves, adapt along with it. This piece was partially influenced by the rich harmonies of my favorite *a cappella* gospel group, Take 6.

FROM THE COMPOSER

The very first thing I do when planning a trip is research the area's best museums and art exhibitions. Museums have always enchanted me; often the building itself is an artistic masterpiece. I tend to react intensely when viewing striking pieces of art—sometimes I imagine Rousseau, Degas, or van Gogh personally connecting with me via the simplest of brushstrokes. These masterpieces never fail to transport me into different eras and corners of the world.

The six piano pieces in this collection were inspired by some of my favorite art pieces. Even though some were more challenging to write than others, I loved the entire process of getting these compositions down on paper. It is my hope that you will appreciate them too.

Warm regards,

Naoko Ikeda

Valse Innocent

Naoko Ikeda

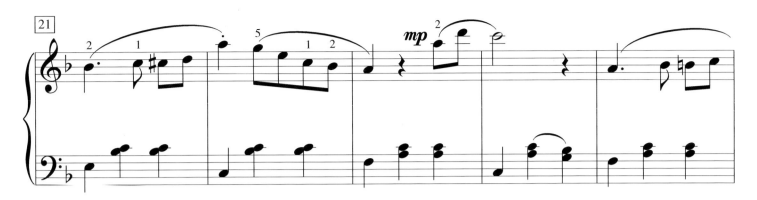

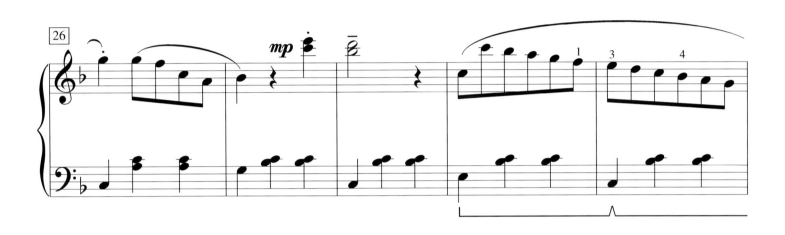

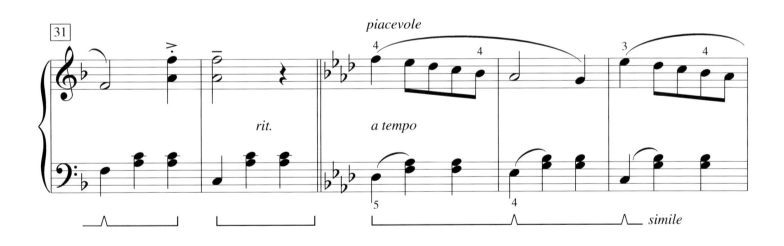

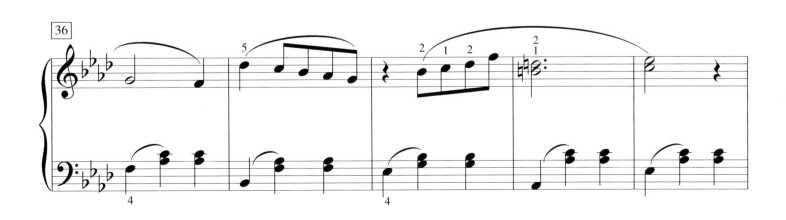

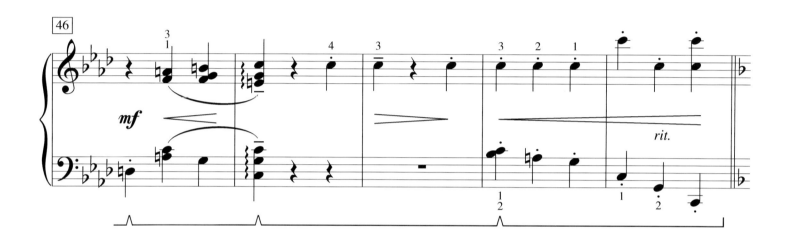

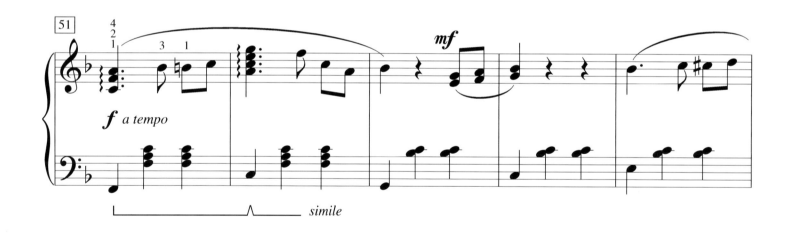

The Jungle

Naoko Ikeda

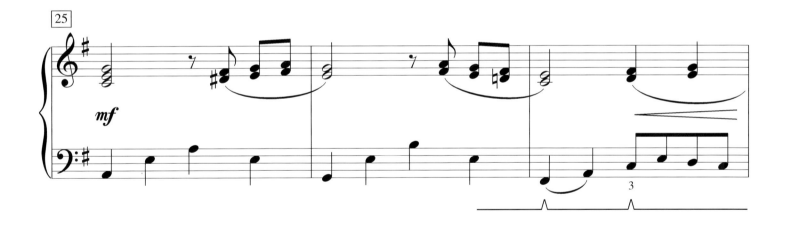

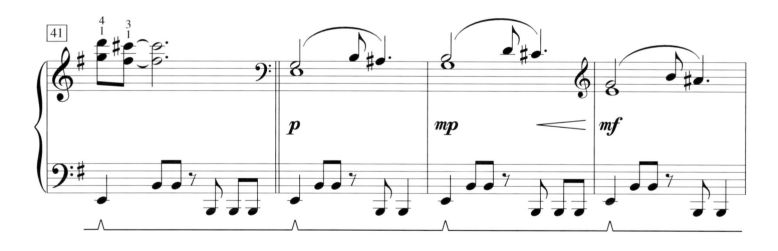

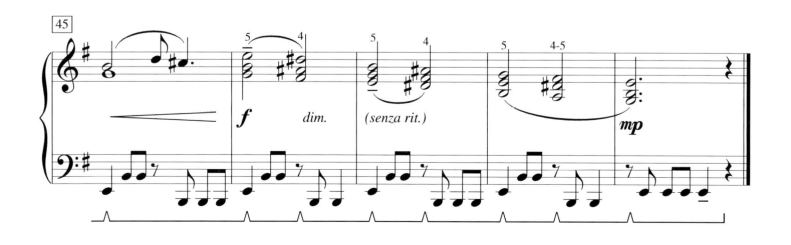

Danse en rose

Naoko Ikeda

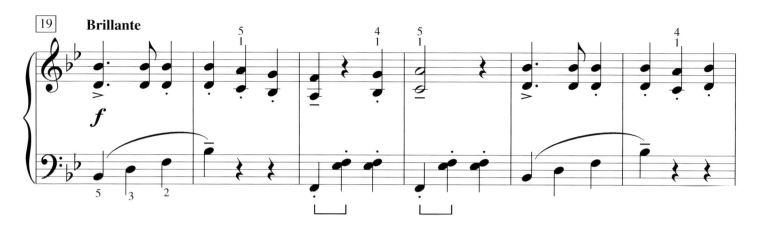

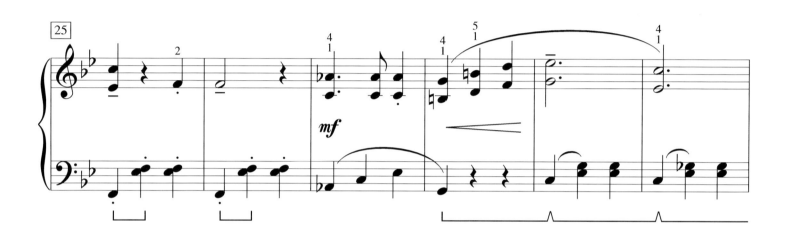

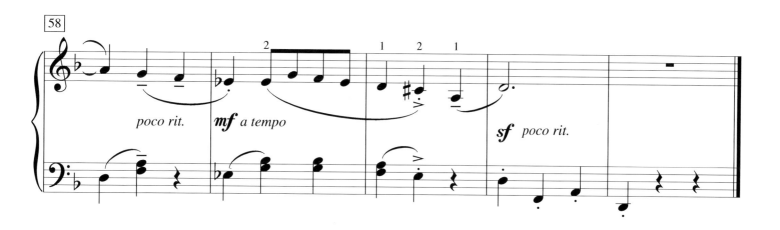

Nocturne of the Stars

Naoko Ikeda

Joyful Love

Naoko Ikeda

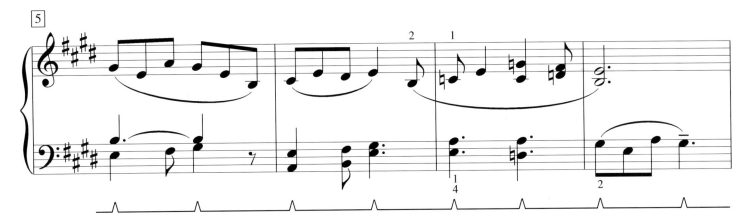

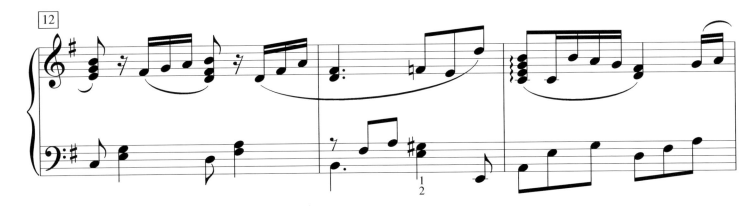

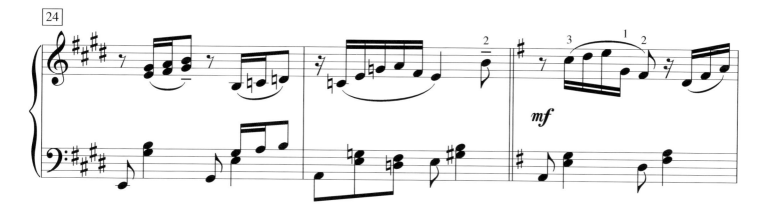

Meno mosso

Dreamy Hues

Naoko Ikeda

22

CLASSIC PIANO REPERTOIRE

The *Classic Piano Repertoire* series includes popular as well as lesser-known pieces from a select group of composers out of the Willis piano archives. Every piece has been newly engraved and edited with the aim to preserve each composer's original intent and musical purpose.

WILLIAM GILLOCK – ELEMENTARY
8 Great Piano Solos
Dance in Ancient Style • Little Flower Girl of Paris • On a Paris Boulevard • Rocking Chair Blues • Sliding in the Snow • Spooky Footsteps • A Stately Sarabande • Stormy Weather.
00416957 ....$8.99

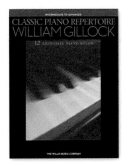

WILLIAM GILLOCK – INTERMEDIATE TO ADVANCED
12 Exquisite Piano Solos
Classic Carnival • Etude in A Major (The Coral Sea) • Etude in E Minor • Etude in G Major (Toboggan Ride) • Festive Piece • A Memory of Vienna • Nocturne • Polynesian Nocturne • Sonatina in Classic Style • Sonatine • Sunset • Valse Etude.
00416912 .... $12.99

EDNA MAE BURNAM – ELEMENTARY
8 Great Piano Solos
The Clock That Stopped • The Friendly Spider • A Haunted House • New Shoes • The Ride of Paul Revere • The Singing Cello • The Singing Mermaid • Two Birds in a Tree.
00110228 ....$8.99

EDNA MAE BURNAM – INTERMEDIATE TO ADVANCED
13 Memorable Piano Solos
Butterfly Time • Echoes of Gypsies • Hawaiian Leis • Jubilee! • Longing for Scotland • Lovely Senorita • The Mighty Amazon River • Rumbling Rumba • The Singing Fountain • Song of the Prairie • Storm in the Night • Tempo Tarantelle • The White Cliffs of Dover.
00110229 .... $12.99

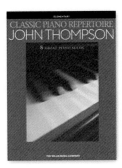

JOHN THOMPSON – ELEMENTARY
9 Great Piano Solos
Captain Kidd • Drowsy Moon • Dutch Dance • Forest Dawn • Humoresque • Southern Shuffle • Tiptoe • Toy Ships • Up in the Air.
00111968 ....$8.99

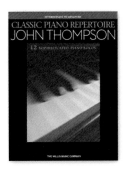

JOHN THOMPSON – INTERMEDIATE TO ADVANCED
12 Masterful Piano Solos
Andantino (from Concerto in D Minor) • The Coquette • The Faun • The Juggler • Lagoon • Lofty Peaks • Nocturne • Rhapsody Hongroise • Scherzando in G Major • Tango Carioca • Valse Burlesque • Valse Chromatique.
00111969 .... $12.99

LYNN FREEMAN OLSON – EARLY TO LATER ELEMENTARY
14 Great Piano Solos
Caravan • Carillon • Come Out! Come Out! (Wherever You Are) • Halloween Dance • Johnny, Get Your Hair Cut! • Jumping the Hurdles • Monkey on a Stick • Peter the Pumpkin Eater • Pony Running Free • Silent Shadows • The Sunshine Song • Tall Pagoda • Tubas and Trumpets • Winter's Chocolatier.
00294722 ....$9.99

LYNN FREEMAN OLSON – EARLY TO MID-INTERMEDIATE
13 Distinctive Piano Solos
Band Wagon • Brazilian Holiday • Cloud Paintings • Fanfare • The Flying Ship • Heroic Event • In 1492 • Italian Street Singer • Mexican Serenade • Pageant Dance • Rather Blue • Theme and Variations • Whirlwind.
00294720 ....$9.99

CLOSER LOOK View sample pages and hear audio excerpts online at **www.halleonard.com**

www.willispianomusic.com

www.facebook.com/willispianomusic